this book belongs to

Maddie and Cece

Be Your Own Parker!
Dana Fonask

© 2017 Dana Fonash

Printed in the United States of America

All rights reserved. This publication is protected by Copyright,
and permission should be obtained from the publisher prior to any prohibited reproduction, storage in a retrieval system, or transmission in any form or by any means, electronic, mechanical, photocopying, recording, or likewise.

Published by
Inner Child Press, ltd.
202 Wiltree Court,
State College, PA 16801, USA

For information regarding permission, write to:
Rights and Permissions Department,
Inner Child Press International
intouch@innerchildpress.com

Library of Congress Cataloging-in-Publication Data Perfectly Imperfect Parker by Dana Fonash, illustrated by Molly Mann Ziegler
p. cm.

3rd Edition

Paperback: ISBN 978-1-952081-57-6
Hard cover: ISBN 978-1-952081-56-9

[1.Christmas- Juvenile Fiction. 2. Self-esteem - Juvenile Fiction.]

Printed on acid-free paper. ∞

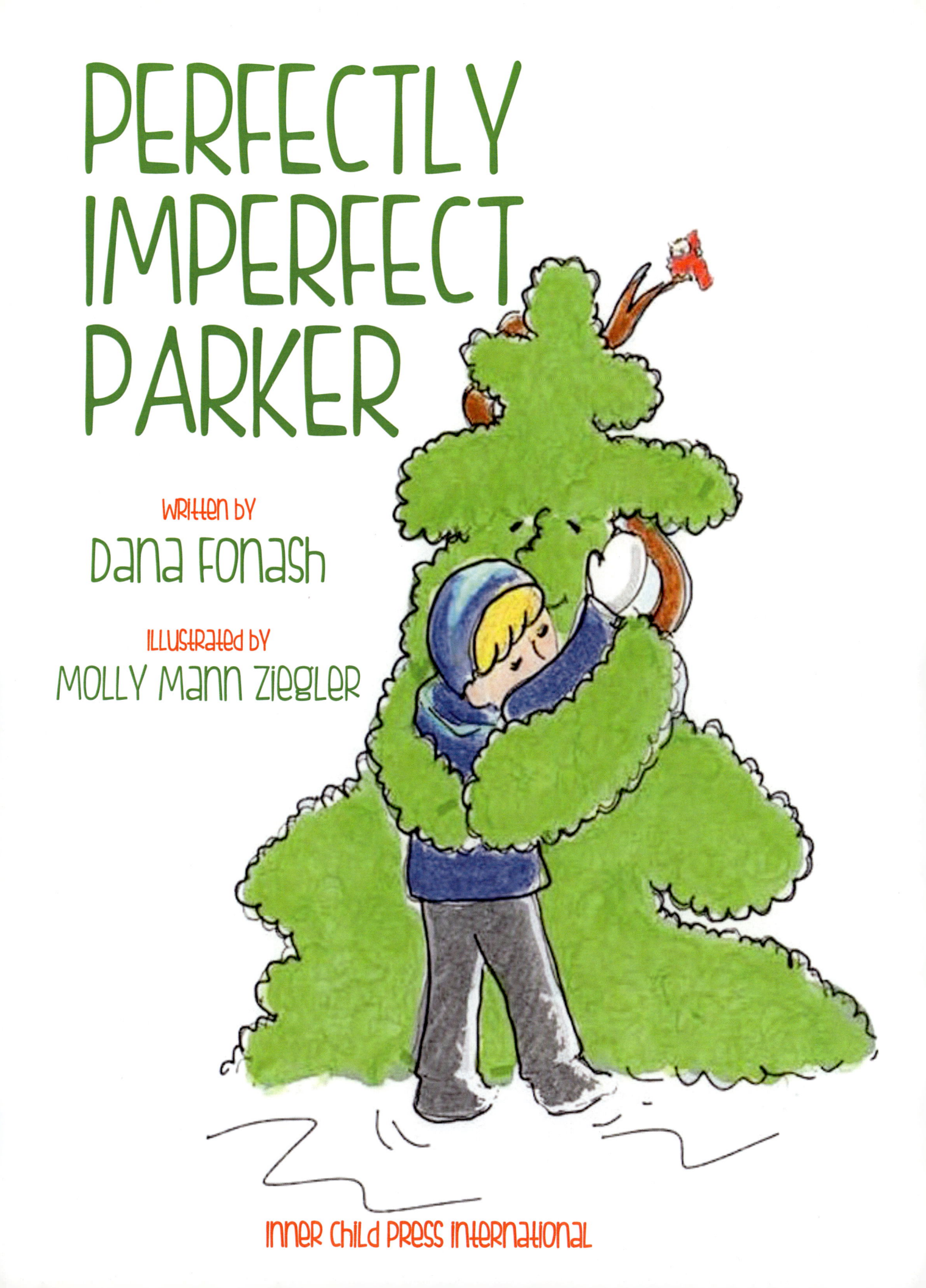

PERFECTLY IMPERFECT PARKER

written by
Dana Fonash

illustrated by
Molly Mann Ziegler

INNER CHILD PRESS INTERNATIONAL

It was a bitterly cold day when the McMillen family set out for the tree farm to find their Christmas tree. The car came to a stop in front of the old barn that housed beautiful handmade wreaths. The family could instantly catch the fragrance of the freshly cut trees. The scent told the nose it was the holiday season.

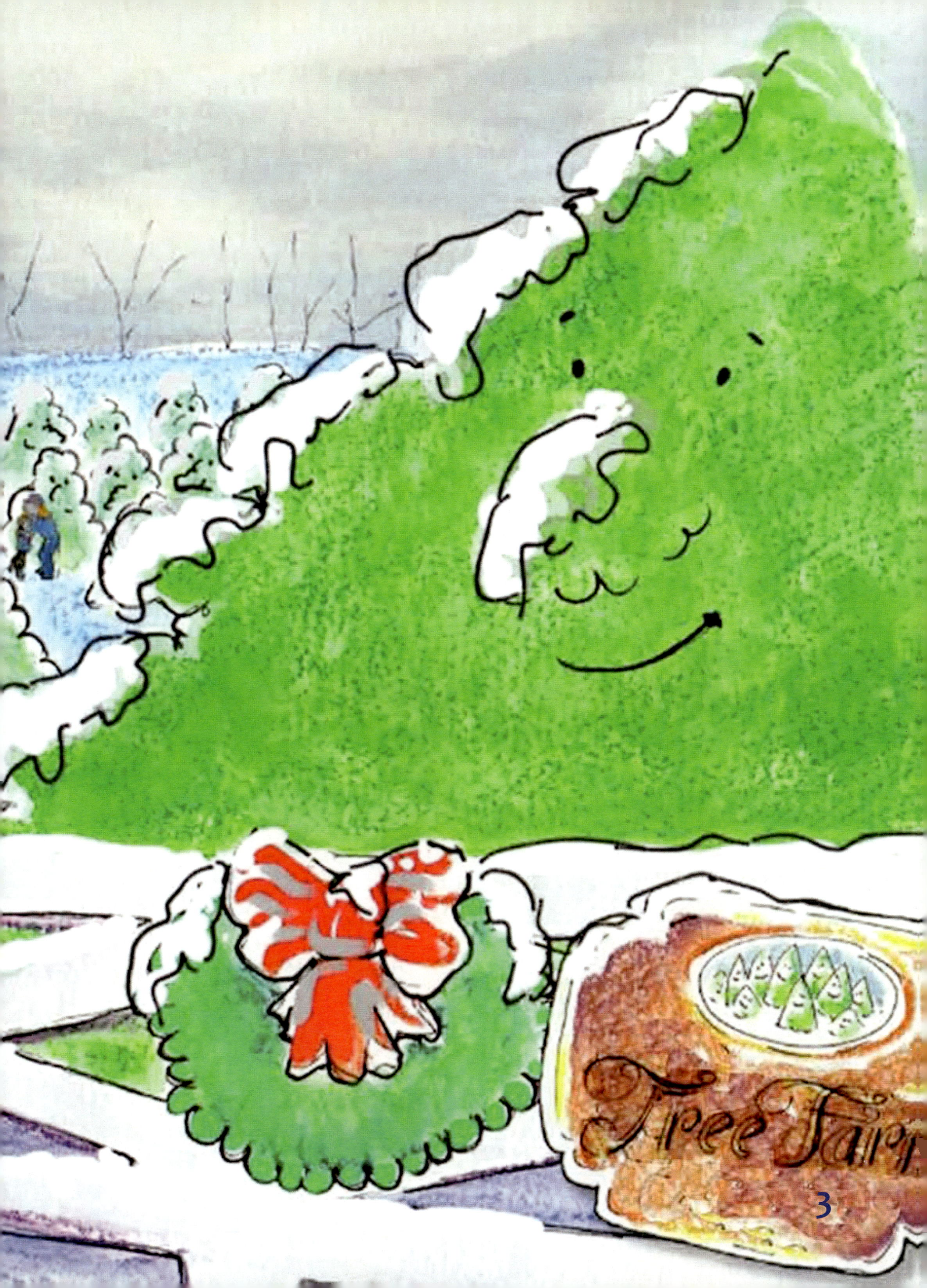
Tree Far

"I'll race you, Nina!" cried Alec as he zipped past his sister down the perfectly aligned aisle of trees. With Dad pulling the tree dolly, the hunt for the best tree was underway.

5

"Ooh, I like this one!" shouted Mom, as the rest of the family circled around. "Okay, this one looks good. Let's keep it in mind kids," announced Dad as he marched on, trying to match Mom by finding a perfect tree of his own for his entry into the annual family tree-picking contest.

7

Alec, the youngest, meandered through the neat rows of anxious trees, who were all hoping to be picked for Christmas. He was on the hunt for the winning tree, and he had already decided he would name it Parker, according to their family tree-naming tradition.

Alec couldn't hear the tall spruces, who were all doing the best they could to appear full, robust, and fragrant.

Mighty Towering Timbers whispered, "Quick, here comes a little boy, this could be our chance . . . straighten up, fellas."

Shady Spruce and Prickly Pine quickly stood at attention, trying to make each of their branches look as straight and beautiful as possible.

Peeking out from behind the others, crooked old Gangly Fir knew this routine all too well. He had a giant hole on one side where his branches hadn't sprouted, so he was sure he was doomed to spend his whole life in a field.

He longed for that moment he had witnessed over and over again for years, when a family picks a tree and gives it a real name. His best friend, Noble Fir, was one of the first trees selected last Christmas season.

Gangly Fir would never forget it, even though it happened so fast and with such celebration that Noble Fir almost missed it herself.

A young family had zeroed in on the sheer beauty of his dear friend as soon as they entered the farm. Noble Fir knew this was her family as they announced her new name: Elsa.

Gangly Fir longed for a family and a real name, but he had concluded that it would never happen with the way he looked. He remembered how, years ago, he had come very close to going home with a family.

They seemed not to mind the gap in his branches . . . until the dad noticed his crooked trunk. And that was that.

13

So, naturally, Gangly Fir almost didn't notice when the little boy approached him. Then he suddenly got that sensation he was so longing for, the feeling of being appreciated, of being wanted.

He started shaking from excitement and hoped the boy, who quite intently was walking all around him, would mistake his quivers for a sudden breeze.

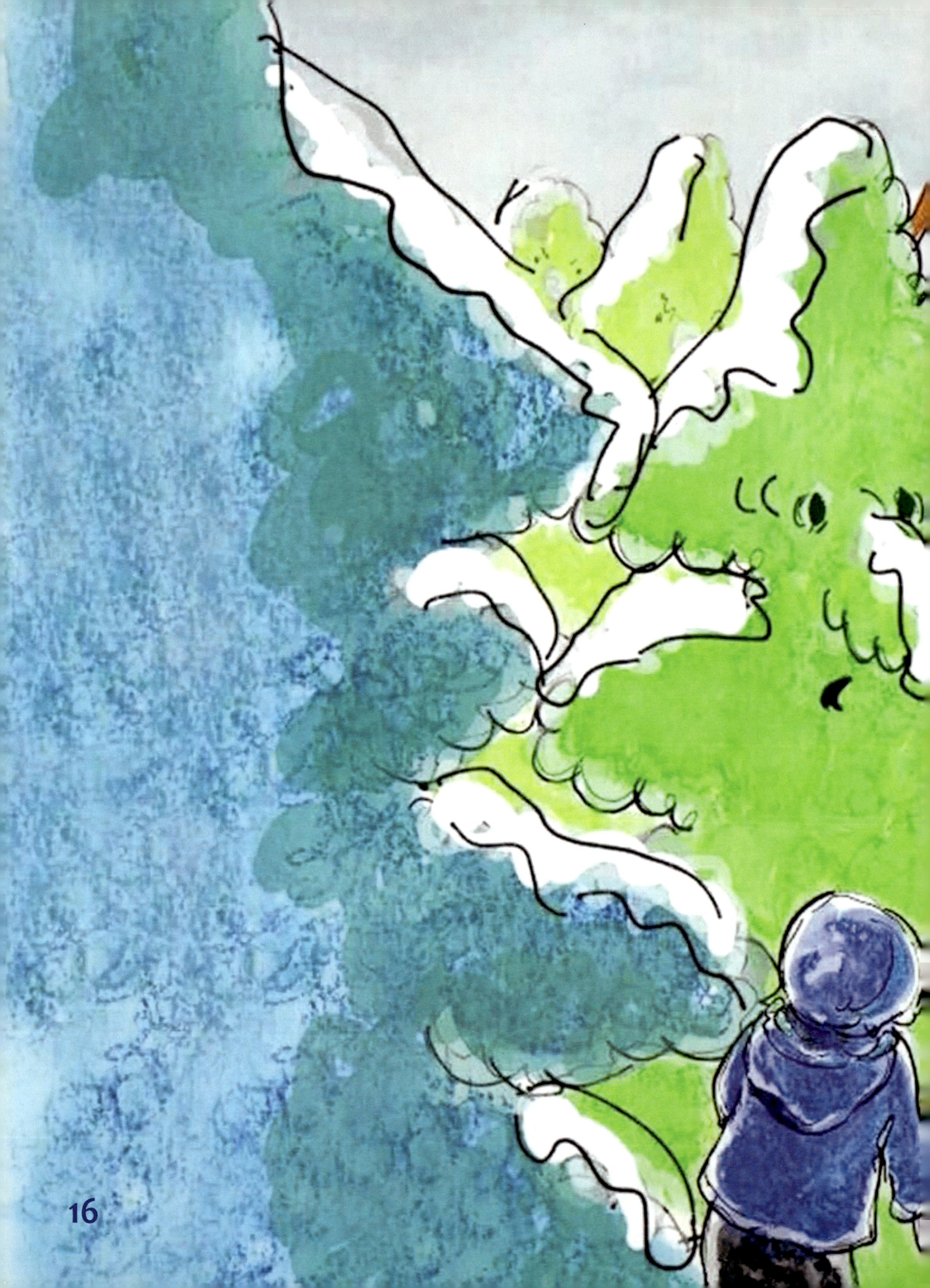

"Ha, you think that boy is seriously considering taking you home?" sneered Towering Timbers with a deep, barking chuckle. "That idea is almost as crooked as your trunk!"

Gangly Fir could hear the quiet laughter of the trees around him. Still, he knew he would make a wonderful Christmas tree – he just needed someone to give him a chance. He hoped this was it.

"Mom, Dad, Nina – I found our tree!" shouted Alec from down the aisle, right in front of snickering Woody Trunk and Prickly Pine. At that moment all the trees fell silent.

They felt that Alec meant what he said. As his mother arrived hurriedly at the spot, Alec said confidently, "Mom, I'd like you to meet this year's tree, Parker. Parker, this is my mom. She'll be the one watering you."

20

"Oh, honey, this tree has a big hole over on this side, and don't you see it has missing branches?" Mom said to Alec gently.

As Mom pointed to his bare section, Gangly Fir felt as though a dagger was digging deep into his crooked trunk. Alec would surely agree, he thought, and his branches began to droop.

When Dad and Nina arrived at the scene a few moments later, Nina laughed at her brother for his ridiculous choice.

"Alec, you are wasting time with your jokes. This tree is bizarre . . . imagine taking our Christmas picture with this tree?"

It was one thing to be teased by his fellow trees, but another to hear insults from people . . . well, it hurt much more.

But Alec walked two paces away from Gangly Fir, turned to his parents, and settled in to make his argument.

"Mom, Dad, you are always telling us how being a little different is a good thing – that our differences make us special. This tree is just that. Who says we have to have a tree that has all perfect sides with a perfect trunk? Are there rule books we have to follow?" Nina first laughed at the idea of rule books for Christmas trees.

Then it 'clicked' in her head what her brother was trying to say. She suddenly joined Alec's side.

"I get it. He's right. This tree may be a bit crooked,
but its imperfections make it perfect.
It's special, unique, and full of character.
It is a tree to remember.

At this point, Gangly Fir was filled with such joy that he thought he was going to pop right out of the ground and do a happy dance. "No, no, I must remain calm. I have gotten close before and failed miserably." The other trees watched in suspense.

27

"Well, kids, it looks like we have found a perfectly imperfect Parker, who might look a bit different than the others but still is just as deserving of a loving home this Christmas. Not only have you two made an excellent decision, but we are also impressed that you were actually paying attention all these years when we talked about accepting others who are different. He and Mom had a good laugh and then said together, "This is it."

Dad then gave Alec a wink as if to say: I am proud of you.

Alec and Nina jumped for joy. Nina cartwheeled all around the newly named Parker while Alec fist-pumped the air. Parker couldn't believe it. He had found a family who not only accepted him for his flaws, but actually liked him for his differences. They weren't 'flaws' at all, it seemed; they were character traits. He had never felt so special in his entire life.

While they prepared him for his journey home, he started dreaming about his new life. He wondered if his new family would wrap him in white or colorful lights.

30

He couldn't wait to see the star they would put on top! He promised himself he would make the McMillen family proud.

On the trek back to the car, Parker couldn't help but smile after hearing a family walk right on past Prickly Pine, saying, "Nah, we want a tree that is a little different. We want a tree that has character."

~ the end ~